Antonio Beato

Collection of photographs of Egypt and Nubia

Antonio Beato

Collection of photographs of Egypt and Nubia

ISBN/EAN: 9783743427655

Manufactured in Europe, USA, Canada, Australia, Japa

Cover: Foto ©Thomas Meinert / pixelio.de

Manufactured and distributed by brebook publishing software
(www.brebook.com)

Antonio Beato

Collection of photographs of Egypt and Nubia

Antonio Beato

Collection of Photographs of Egypt and Nubia

[Between 1860 - 1900]

Brooklyn
Museum
Libraries and
Archives

Ramesseum : Vue d'ensemble

Karnak Luxor

unleserlich

De vetusta Stele

Monument Hole.

A. Beato

....

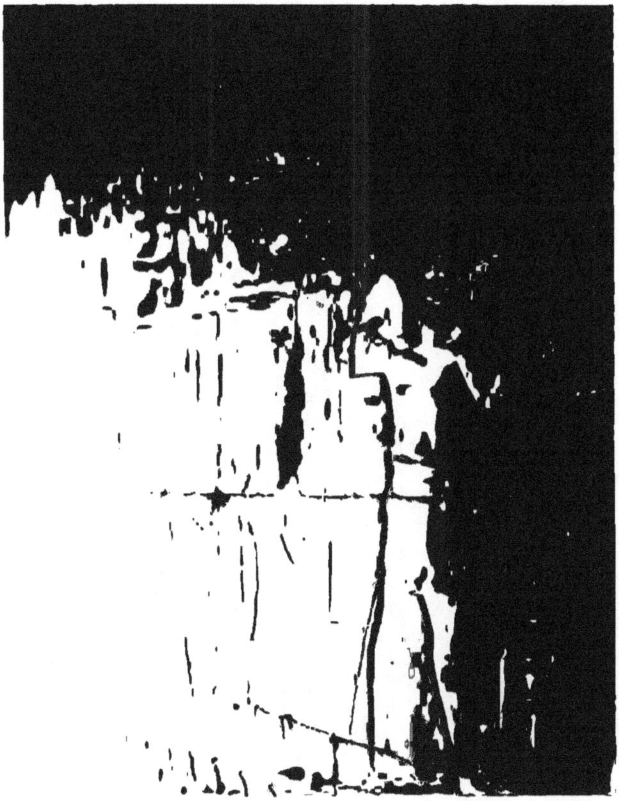

Der el Medineh. 1901

Street scene — *1951*

Ancient Cairo, Egypt

Medinet Habu   fragments of the [illegible]

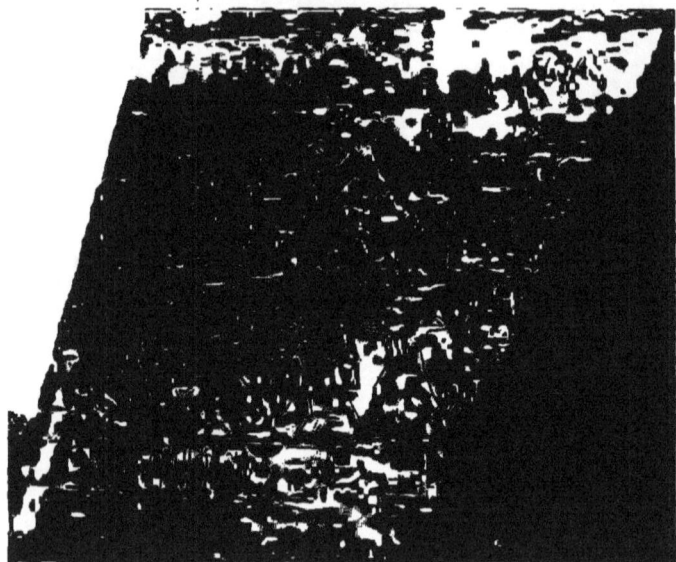

Medinet Habu

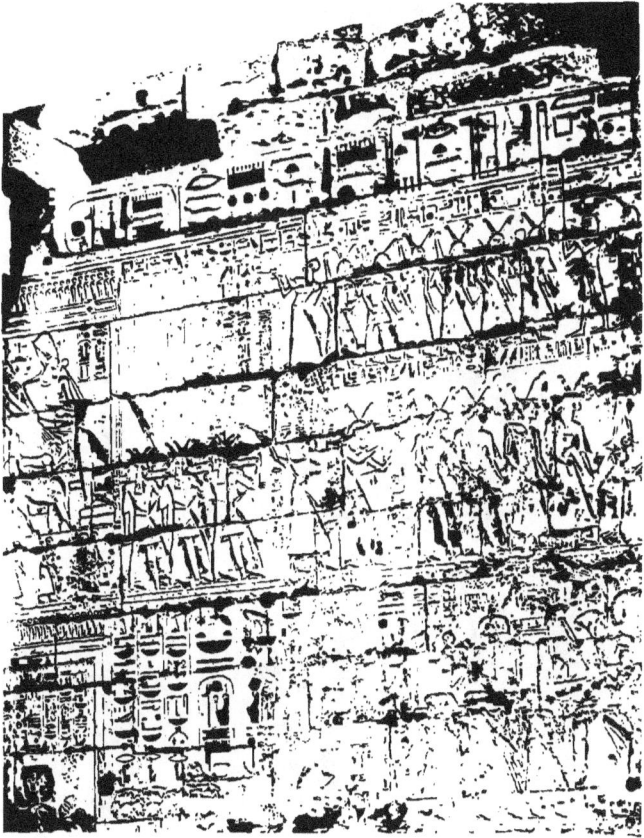

Medinet Habu. R.

I le At rel Eabre: Presenciey Rai

the rich statues so on t

Korwar. Geelvinck A.

Stewart: Using the Camera at Will

Kavak Collection

Kasimir Malewitsch

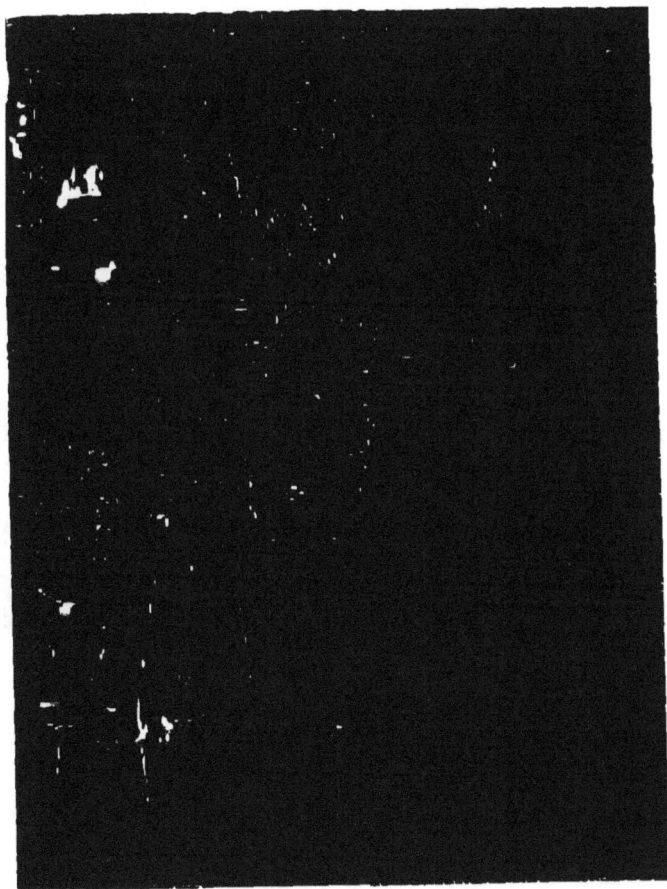

das originale Seee   t. M.

Common violets of the...

A. Beato

Marcot jur.

Karte 5.

Rameau s'en retour fille brûlée

térier ... selle selected ad

No count ... het hee ... all

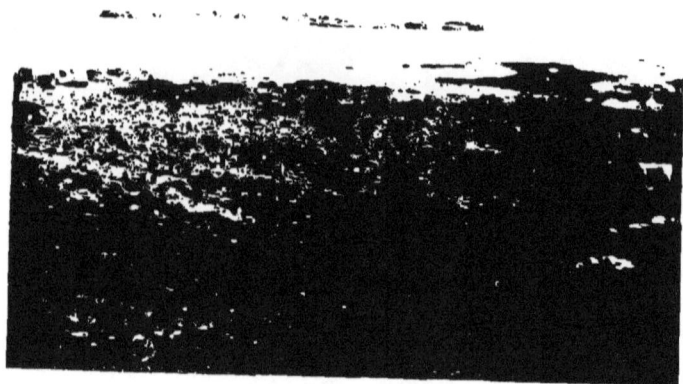

Maria sembra una...

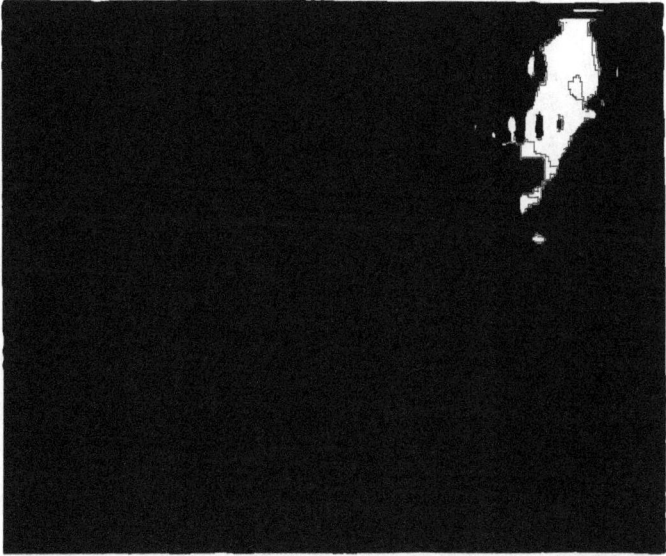

Aurora borealis

Kirwa: Tomb of Seddss Trill

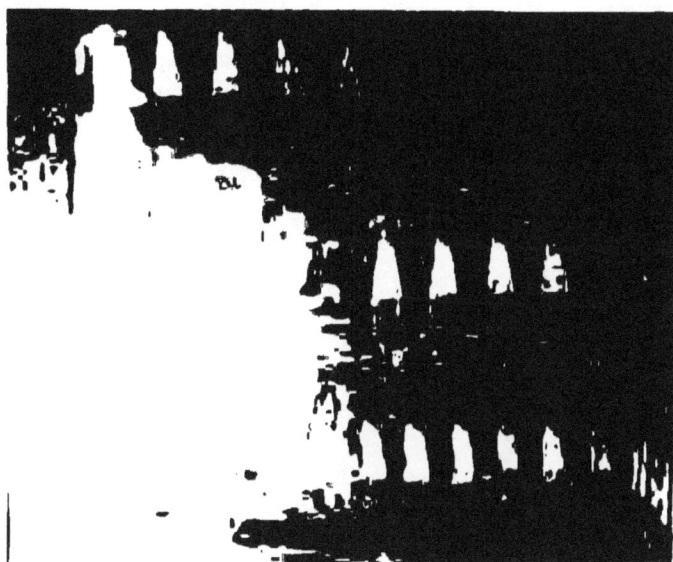

Leben ist mehr Leben

June 16

Index:

www.ingramcontent.com/pod-product-compliance
Lightning Source LLC
Chambersburg PA
CBHW021535270326
41930CB00008B/1261